W9-CUY-205

Traditional Chinese Residences

"Culture of China" Editorial Board:

Consultants: Cai Mingzhao, Zhao Changqian, Huang Youyi and Liu Zhibin
Chief Editor: Xiao Xiaoming
Board Members: Xiao Xiaoming, Li Zhenguo, Tian Hui, Hu Baomin,
               Fang Yongming, Hu Kaimin, Cui Lili and Lan Peijin

Editor: Jia Xianfeng
Written by: Wang Qijun and Jia Xianfeng
Translated by: Zhang Shaoning
English Text Editor: Wang Zengfen
Photographers: Wang Qijun, Lan Peijin, Sun Shuming, Cheng Weidong,
               Li Zhisen, Yu Zhiyong and Sun Jianping
Layout Designer: Tang Shaowen
Cover Designer: Cai Rong

First Edition 2002

Traditional Chinese Residences
ISBN 7-119-03041-8

© Foreign Languages Press
Published by Foreign Languages Press
24 Baiwanzhuang Road, Beijing 100037, China
Home Page: http://www.flp.com.cn
E-mail Addresses: info@flp.com.cn
               sales@flp.com.cn
Printed in the People's Republic of China

Traditional Chinese Residences

By Wang Qijun

Foreign Languages Press   Beijing

Contents

Major Architectural Forms of Chinese Residences   017

A Survey of Traditional Chinese Residences

In prehistoric times, dwellings were crude, and tended to be similar in design the world over; they differed only in the availability of local building materials and the topography they had to adapt to.

As the techniques of production improved, the styles of clothing, cuisine, transportation, etc. of different peoples gradually took on their own national colors and cultural characteristics. The same was true for the shelters that people built to dwell in, and a wide diversity of styles formed all over the world. Chinese residences, in particular, occupy a unique place in the history of world architecture.

The Development of Traditional Chinese Residences

In the remote past people lived in caves, and under trees and crags. Six to seven thousand years ago, when the matriarchal society was in its prime, large houses were built to accommodate all the members of a clan. Archaeologists have discovered several thousand relics of residential buildings of that period, which can be divided into northern and southern types.

The northern type, represented by the building relics of the Yangshao culture, features semi-underground, shallow caves with cone-shaped or reversed V-shaped roofs made of wood and straw, or underground caves.

The southern type, represented by the building relics of the Hemudu culture, features wooden or bamboo houses built on stilts.

In the Shang Dynasty, over three millennia ago, according to records inscribed on bones and tortoise shells, the walls of buildings were made of earth compressed between wooden boards. In the Western Zhou Dynasty (c. 1100-771 B.C.), the

The caves found near Yangshao Village in Mianchi County, Henan Province, are the earliest dwellings of the Yangshao Culture (5,000 to 7,000 years ago) known so far. The primitive people dug these calabash-shaped caves in the ground with stone tools. They were entered from the surface. Erosion over centuries has revealed the longitudinal sections of the caves.

The typical semi-underground dwelling of a family during the period of patriarchal society 5,000 years ago was built with earth and wood, with a fire pit in the center. The small window in the roof lets in light, ventilates the dwelling, and lets out smoke from the cooking fire. The dwelling in the picture is a reconstruction made by modern scholars.

earthen walls of some buildings were covered with bricks on the outside. Imperial palaces, ancestral temples of the imperial family and aristocrats' homes were roofed with plate or semicircular-shaped tiles, marking important progress in ancient Chinese architecture. The earliest courtyard houses known so far also came into being in that period. Remains of pottery drainpipes have been found in ruins of buildings dating from Western Zhou.

During the Spring and Autumn and Warring States periods (772-221 BC), residential buildings and palaces already had arches over gateways and double-eaved roofs. Some windows were decorated with crossed latticework. The floor inside a house of that time was separated from the ground outside by a wide space. One took off one's shoes before entering a house, and sat on the floor. The buildings of the Warring States Period are marked by decorative roof tiles featuring a mythical beast called *taotie*, and swirl and cloud patterns in relief.

Multi-storied buildings were in fashion during the Han Dynasty, which are far different from the residences of later ages. As the wooden frame technology had matured, and wood materials were easy to acquire, people of that time built many multi-storied buildings. The picture shows a funeral object in the shape of a model building in the collection of the Xuzhou Museum in Jiangsu Province. It has low eaves and a roofed courtyard.

The ancient city of Jiaohe in the Turpan Depression, Xinjiang Uygur Autonomous Region, remains as it was in the Tang Dynasty. The picture shows the ruins of residences around a large courtyard.

Geomancy, known in Chinese as *fengshui*, took shape in China during the Qin and Han dynasties (221 BC-AD 220). Based on the theories of *qi* (vital energy), *yin-yang* (opposite forces) and the five elements (earth, air, fire, wood and water), and using the Eight Diagrams of the *Book of Changes* as a means of divination, geomancers would choose what was considered the ideal place to situate a building.

In the Han Dynasty, especially the Western Han Dynasty (206 BC-AD 24), the most common type of residential building consisted of one hall and two bedrooms. A "bedroom" was about 11 square meters, and a "hall" was twice the size of a bedroom. The layout of such a house, together with its yard, was a square.

Korean dwelling houses maintain the general characteristics of Tang Dynasty residences. The picture shows a Korean house in Longjing County in the Yanbian Korean Autonomous Prefecture, Jilin Province.

Quite different from the northern residential buildings of later years, storied buildings were in vogue during the Han Dynasty. Some manor houses of that time included a watchtower, which contained a drum to be beaten in case of danger.

It was not until the period of the Five Dynasties (907-960) that ordinary Chinese people gradually stopped sitting on the floor, and adopted chairs and other forms of furniture for their houses. Basically, all types of furniture used in later ages could be found in that period.

The rulers of the Tang Dynasty (618-907) introduced the community-precinct system into their cities. A precinct was a group of residential buildings surrounded by walls on the four sides. Outside the walls were streets. A large precinct had a gate in each wall, while smaller ones only had gates in the east and west walls.

Each residential building in a community or precinct was also surrounded by high walls. So a residential building was protected by at least three walls: the city wall, the precinct wall and the courtyard wall. Within the courtyard wall were more yards and walls, and one had to pass the outer gate, middle gate, hall, etc., before reaching the bedrooms. This system was abolished during the Northern Song Dynasty (960-1127).

Ancient Chinese residential buildings followed a strict hierarchical system. According to the *History of the Song Dynasty*, "The home of a prince in office is called *fu*, that of an official is called *zhai*, and that of a commoner is called *jia*." Specific stipulations were given on the size and form of the dwellings at each hierarchical level.

In the Song Dynasty (960-1279), the entrance to the house of an aristocrat or high official often had three bays, through the middle one of which carriages and horses could pass. Rooms were built along the sides of the courtyard in place of the Tang-dynasty porches, enlarging the living space. The layout of aristocrats' residences followed the Han Dynasty tradition of "hall at the front and bedrooms at the rear." The hall and bedrooms were connected by corridors. The accumulation of furnishings made houses higher and narrower.

Song Dynasty buildings had the distinct architectural characteristics known as *juzhe* (raising and depression), *shengqi* (rise) and *cejiao* (batter). As a straight gable roof would look dull, *juzhe* was to give the pitched roof a concave curvature, and *shengqi* was to keep the ridge and eave of the central bay level, while creating a graceful curvature of the eave line and roof ridge toward the corners of the building. *Cejiao* was to slant the columns of a building towards the center.

Drawing lines linking the columns at the upper and lower ends respectively, one could see that all the columns lean towards the central point. Such a building looks narrower toward the top. Folk buildings with the above characteristics were more stable, and looked more elegant in general.

Ming Dynasty (1368-1644) residences were much larger than those of the previous ages. As the patriarchal clan system was prevalent at this time, there were many large families of three or four generations, and all disputes within the clan were settled in the clan hall. Many examples of Ming residences still exist today, some of them very large in scale. In that period, with the development of brick making, brick residences took up a larger proportion than before. Although there were still many timber structures, the wooden columns were enclosed in brick walls. This brought about a change in the exterior of ordinary residences: Elevations emphasized the beauty of brick structures instead of wooden structures.

Although the Ming Dynasty followed the traditional hierarchical system of residences, many high officials, rich merchants and landlords ignored it. According to records, some of them had houses containing up to 1,000 rooms and splendid gardens, and covering an area of several square kilometers. The extant Ming residences, such as that of Lu, a bureaucrat-landlord, in Dongyang, Zhejiang Province, after management of several generations, were large, majestic and splendidly decorated complexes. The extant Ming residences in Shexian and Yixian counties of Anhui Province are famous for their gorgeous decorations far exceeding the relevant provisions for residences in the *History of the Ming Dynasty*.

The earliest apartment buildings known so far are also from the Ming Dynasty. The oval-shaped Qiyun Building in Shangping Village, Hua'an County, Fujian Province, was built in the 18th year of the reign of Emperor Wanli (1590). The round Shengping Building with enclosing granite walls, located in the same area, was built in the 29th year of the reign of Wanli (1601). They both have a main courtyard in the center, and 20-odd apartments, each with its own kitchen, small courtyard, hall, bedrooms, drawing room and staircase. According to the clan records, the history of the Qiyun Building can be traced back to the fourth year of the reign of Emperor Hongwu (1371). In other words, China had apartment buildings as early as 600 years ago.

The Qing Dynasty (1644-1911) saw a great development in building techniques, such as earth ramming, glazing, carpentry and brick arch building. However, there was no breakthrough or innovation in the architectural form of ordinary residences. From the middle of the Ming Dynasty to the Opium War in 1840, the commodity economy grew, and the class

Qing Dynasty residences are found in large numbers throughout China. The picture shows the gorgeously decorated interior of the Qing Dynasty Chengzhi Hall, in Hongcun Village, Yixian County, Anhui Province.

of merchants grew wealthier. The latter pursued affluence and artistic beauty, which is reflected in the sometimes excessive stress on decoration in their homes.

In Zhangzhou Prefecture, Fujian Province, round earthen buildings occur in peculiar shapes. The Eryi Building, over 200 years old, has a common round shape but ingenious interior design. This is a bird's-eye view of the building from the top of a nearby hill.

In the history of Chinese residences, many innovations were made in the wooden framework and shapes of houses during the Song, Jin and Yuan dynasties. The crescent beam, broken threshold of the entrance house, asymmetrical connection of roof trusses, layouts formed with verandas, and so on, brought about variety to architectural styles. However, the forms of wooden frameworks of folk residences in the Ming and Qing dynasties tended to be more simple and fixed. In the Central Plains, many residences built in those dynasties, lacking the gentle curvature of the roof line, display a more serious, restrained and solemn style. During the reigns of the Qing emperors Kangxi and Yongzheng, in particular, expensive houses were fully decorated with carvings, from architraves to gate piers. The gables were decorated with fine, intricate carvings, and the verandas had walls of polished brick at both ends. In southern areas, fire-blocking gables in various shapes gave an effect of luxury and elegance. And in northern areas, the inner gates in traditional

compound houses were painted in rich colors. Although the carvings and other decorations are sometimes criticized as over-elaborate, Qing dwellings display far more advanced architectural techniques than those of previous ages. A lot of examples of Qing Dynasty residences still remain, some of them perfectly preserved.

From pre-Qin times to the beginning of the 20th century, the basic features of Chinese buildings remained the same, in spite of changes in architectural styles in different dynasties and areas. A wooden framework was the main part of the structure, and there was usually a group of single buildings.

The Artistic Features of Traditional Chinese Residences

Proper Layout: The Void Accompanied by the Solid

Just as in traditional Chinese painting, so in traditional Chinese buildings—spacing is one of the most important principles. Standing on a stone arch bridge in a small town south of the Yangtze River, one can see the spacing principle in the layout of the dense roofs and white walls. As a saying goes, "Density to the point of impermeableness, and emptiness to the point of allowing horses to gallop through." It is the

Residences along the Tuojiang River in Fenghuang (Phoenix) County, Hunan Province.

beauty of contrast. Density and emptiness should be arranged properly. In addition, the roofs of traditional buildings are arranged unevenly to avoid monotonousness, and the rhythmic undulation of the roof is often reflected in the walls. This "void accompanied by solid" principle holds a unique place in the history of architectural aesthetics. Large, solid walls, like the white space in Chinese paintings, are decorated with eye-catching doors and windows. The rhythmic variance of the void and the solid gives to a residence a certain charming air of unaffectedness, tranquility and secludedness.

Residence in Hsinchu County, Taiwan Province.

Tranquil Interior Surrounded by Solid Walls, Displaying a Picturesque Tone

Large, solid walls not only function as a protective surrounding defense, they also embody tranquility. Secluding the residence from the outside world, the thick, solid walls block noise from outside and keep the inside quiet.

Unlike Greek architecture, which is an organic combination of blocks, Chinese traditional architecture emphasizes unobstructedness and tone, and displays the rich variance and connotation of the tone with innumerable flowing lines.

The roofing of folk residences in northern Fujian Province maintains a Song Dynasty style: both ends of the roof ridge and the four corners of the roof turn upward, leaving no straight line on the roof. The fire-blocking gable also has curvature on the top. The undulating lines represent a rising and falling rhythm. Standing in green fields, the buildings look graceful and picturesque.

Wuzhen is an ancient town by the Grand Canal in Tongxiang County, Zhejiang Province. There are more waterways than streets, and more boats than cars in the town. Most residences and shops stand by the waterside.

Simplicity, Elegance and Connection Between Exterior and Interior

Partitions such as railings, pierced stonework or brickwork, and window lattices act as frames and agents of distancing. A line of a poem by Chen Jianzhai of the Song Dynasty goes, "Shining are flowers and leaves on the other side of the curtain." Here, the curtain enhances the scene on the other side. Connection between the exterior and the interior is one of the artistic methods used in Chinese architecture. The combination of partition and connection can be achieved with a bamboo curtain, a door or a window. The lattices in partitions, doors and windows make ideal frames, separating the outside scenery into several sections.

In many traditional residences, the interior and exterior penetrate and communicate with each other. Partitions, doors and windows act as intermediaries for the outside and inside scenes. The small window lattices in various shapes let in the bright rays of the sun, which cast their shadows inside like paper-cut works. The outside light and scenery viewed through the lattices are varied. Besides softening the light inside, lattices also give a sense of separation.

Partition and connection represent the principle of the void accompanied by the solid. The ancient Chinese character for "brightness" is a combination of "window" and "moon." So "brightness" means moonlight coming in through the window. It is really a poetic creation. In the exterior design of traditional residences, when the courtyard is large, the architect often partitions it with lattice walls and low walls to create variety and contrast. A long, narrow courtyard can be partitioned into several sections so that one cannot see along the length of it.

Dawn in Ma'anzhai Village, in the Sanjiang Dong Autonomous County, Guangxi Zhuang Autonomous Region.

"Connection" and "transparency," as the opposite of "partition," supplement and are supplemented by the latter too. The use of various types of lattice work gives the building a sense of mystery while still connecting the interior with the exterior.

Simple and elegant beauty is a major feature of the traditional Chinese residence. Most dwellings have no ceilings, and the beams and rafters are exposed. The railing structure shows even the ground floor, accompanied only with some decoration in certain corners. The exterior usually consists of plain brick walls. Wooden eaves are seldom painted, but only coated with tung oil as a damp-proof treatment. Not having to follow set rules, the decoration of the exterior, done in the light of the actual conditions, is simple without being crude.

Brick carvings on the upper part of the lintel of the door of a residence in Zhentou Township, Jixi County, Anhui Province.

Window and door latticework in a residence in Jingdezhen, Jiangxi Province.

Tasteful Decoration in Bright Colors

Other residences, however, are richly decorated without sacrificing elegance. Some large and luxurious ones have exquisitely carved beams, railings decorated with complicated patterns, and brick carvings as elaborately done as those on Shang Dynasty bronze wares. In many residences, brick and wood carvings combine harmoniously. Some dwellings are fully decorated with carvings but give an unaffected and subdued impression.

The Qiaojiabao Mansion in Qixian County, Shanxi Province, is an example of such a style. In addition to rich decoration, the various forms of roofing add elegance to the general scene of refinement.

Poetic and Melodious Beauty

As we entered a small village by Taihu Lake, the murmuring stream led us into a picture as beautiful as a melody.

The arrangement of a residence can be musical, in such aspects as combination of spaces, arrangement of courtyards and structures, and positioning of doors and windows. It is music frozen in time. And the secret of this artistic achievement of the traditional Chinese residence lies in the rich variety of space arrangement.

Major Architectural Forms of Chinese Residences

Chinese Residences

The Courtyard Houses of Beijing

Traditional Chinese residences are mostly buildings arranged around courtyards, and, generally speaking, the courtyard houses used to be the most ideal architectural form. Beijing courtyard houses are the most representative. In a courtyard house, buildings and courtyards in proper sizes are laid out symmetrically along a central axis, showing an orderly atmosphere of the family, and embodying the traditional Chinese ethics of respect for elders.

Screen walls in Beijing courtyard houses can be divided into independent screen walls and screen walls connected with the gate. The picture shows an independent screen wall.

Floral-pendant gate of a residence in Haidian District, Beijing.

Beijing courtyard houses vary in size. The larger ones have several courtyards. The picture shows a bird's-eye view of one of the latter.

The picture shows a floral-pendant gate of a Beijing courtyard house. Servants lived outside the gate while the family lived on the interior.

The windows and interior furnishings in a courtyard house in north China.

Residences in Qixian County, Shanxi Province

The Qiaos' House abounds in decoration. The picture shows the chimneys on top of the roof, which are well decorated despite the fact that nobody can see them clearly from the ground.

Located in the valley of the Fenhe River, Qixian is the most affluent area in Shanxi Province. People of this county have a tradition of engaging in business. During the reigns of emperors Daoguang and Xianfeng (1821-61) in the Qing Dynasty, over a half of the number of households were doing business outside the county. As a result, there were many luxurious houses in the county. Today, over 40 of them are still well preserved. The Qixian residences have three main features of Shanxi residences: First, high surrounding walls. The brick, windowless walls rising as high as a four- or five-story building functions as a strong defense. Second, the main buildings have pent roofs, allowing rainwater to flow towards the courtyard, which implies "no rich water should be let out of one's own fields." Third, the rectangular courtyards are long from north to south while narrow from east to west, and the gate is often positioned in the southeast corner.

The Qiaos' House in Qixian County, Shanxi Province.

The screen wall facing the entrance of the Qiaos' House is known as "Hundred Longevity Screen Wall," as it is carved with 100 forms of the Chinese character meaning "longevity."

Among the many parlors in the Qiaos' House, the main parlor was the place where the host received guests, and held feasts and business discussions.

Having many courtyards, the Qiaos' House also has many gates, each of which has its own characteristics. Their common features are abundant decoration and exquisite carving.

The Qiaos' House, a representative of the traditional rural residences of
Qixian, is a museum of folk culture today. The picture shows the entrance to
one of its five courtyards.

Cave Dwellings

The cave dwelling is one of the exceptions to the traditional Chinese residence, which is mostly a group of wooden structures with courtyards. The cave dwelling is the most distinctive form of abode with the most local colors. It can be divided into three types. The first is constructed by digging horizontally into the loess cliff; the second is built by digging into the ground to make a large courtyard and then digging caves in the walls around it; the third is an earth-sheltered brick house on the ground in the shape of a cave dwelling. The last is the best in the three, and the most costly.

The Yan'an area has the largest number of cave dwellings in China. Even today over 90 percent of the local residences are cave dwellings.

The ingeniously designed screen wall inside the entrance to *Jiang Yaozu's House* has a full-moon-shaped opening and bears exquisite brick carvings.

Millionaire Kang's Manor consists of both buildings and cave
dwellings. What is notable and rare is that all the cave dwellings in the
manor have two stories.

The underground cave dwelling is a peculiar form of Chinese residence.

The interior of a cave dwelling
in Pingyao, Shanxi Province.

A parapet and a fengshui wall in the shape of a screen wall on top of a cave dwelling in Pingyao.

Jiang Yaozu's House has two courtyards, the rear one being nearly three meters higher than the front one.

A water intake outside the kitchen of Jiang Yaozu's House in Mizhi, Shaanxi Province (left).

A drain outside the kitchen of Jiang Yaozu's House (right).

A cave dwelling in Shanxi.

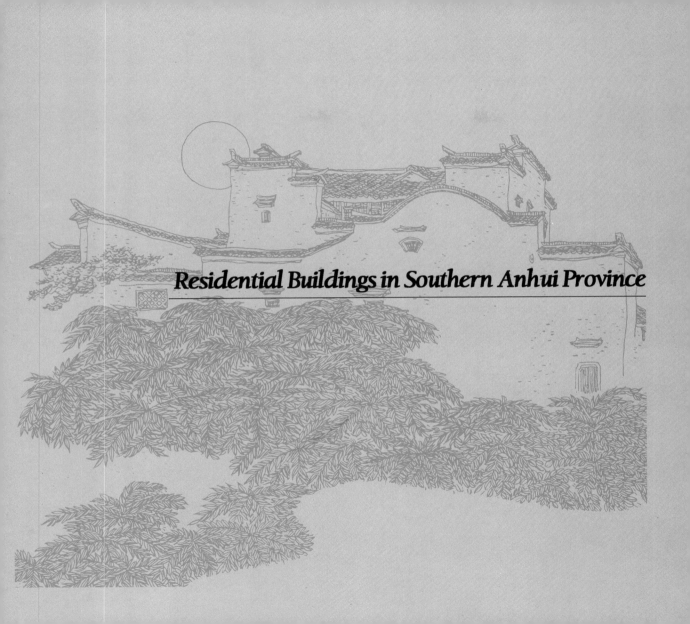

Residential Buildings in Southern Anhui Province

Sitting in verdant mountains and by green waters, the ancient villages of Huizhou have developed into harmonious combinations of natural and artificial scenery through centuries. The artificial tunnels and ponds around the villages, green old trees by waters, and lotuses and flocks of ducks in waters form a beautiful picture. The residences and their reflection in the water give an impression of tranquility and grace. The lanes in this area are flanked by high walls topped with step gables.

The white-walled, black-tiled residences in rural areas of southern Anhui Province present a charming picture.

The layout of Southern Anhui villages is characteristic. Unlike most Chinese villages that face south, the Shijia Village in Jixi County is laid out like a chessboard, and all the residences face north. It was built in the Ming Dynasty by descendents of Shi Shouxin, a general who helped found the Northern Song Dynasty. According to the elderly villagers, they built north-facing houses to commemorate their ancestor Shi Shouxin, who was from Kaifeng in Henan Province in the north.

Most southern Anhui residences are multi-storied. Those built before the Ming Dynasty have a low, crude ground floor and a high, spacious and well-decorated second floor. However, those built in the Qing Dynasty are the opposite, where the well-decorated ground floor contains halls and parlors, and the second floor bedrooms, studies and storerooms.

The half-moon-shaped pool in the center of Hongcun Village in Yixian County reflects the buildings standing by it.

Besides beautiful residences, there are impressive public buildings in villages in southern Anhui. The picture shows the Wind and Rain Bridge in Bei'an Village, Shexian County, of which the windows on the two sides have different shapes.

Residences in Tangmo Village, built along the stream which runs through the center of the village, have protruding low eaves that extend over the street in front of them.

Tangyue Village in Shexian has seven memorial arches. A symbol of great honor in feudal society, an arch would be built when a local person became an official, ranked high in the imperial civil examinations, was over 100 years old, or was acknowledged as a chaste woman. Two of Tangyue's arches were built in the Ming Dynasty, and the other five were built in the Qing Dynasty.

The front building or the first story of many traditional residences serves as a store. The picture shows a Chinese medicine store in the ancient town of Tunxi.

The exquisite woodcarvings in the interior of Qing Dynasty residences in southern Anhui are indicative of the opulence in which the wealthy merchants of that time lived.

A residence in southern Anhui Province may look simple from the outside, but the interior is densely decorated with woodcarvings. Some patterns are simple, and some are complicated. The picture on the left shows the courtyard of a southern Anhui residence, and the picture on the right shows a ceilingless corridor.

The entrance to Tangmo Village in Huizhou was arranged in accordance with fengshui principles, including the arrangement of a garden and the setting up of memorial arches. The picture shows an ancient three-eaved tower in front of the group of buildings and an auspicious tree near it.

Residential Buildings in the Southern Region of Rivers and Lakes

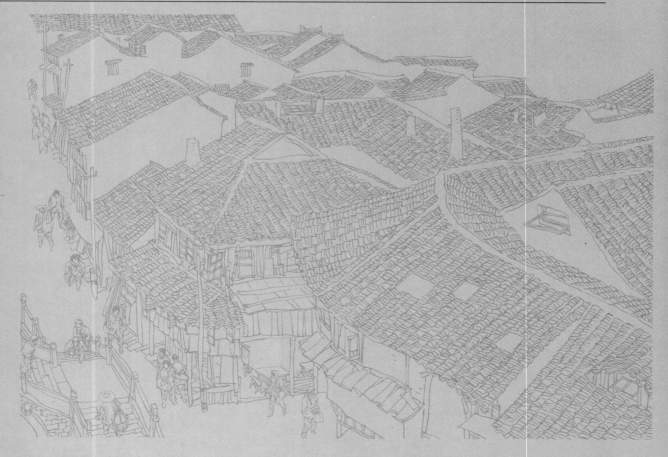

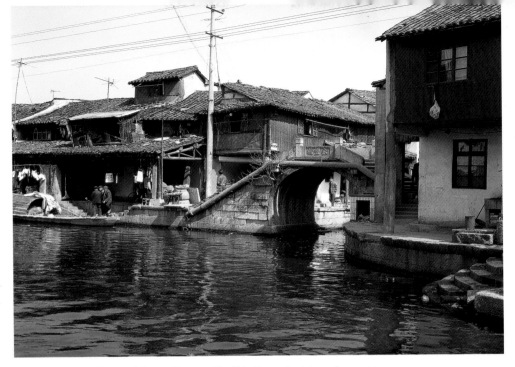

Keqiao Township in Shaoxing, Zhejiang Province. The old building in the picture no longer exists.

The Jiangsu- and Zhejiang-style residences in the Taihu Valley are of high quality in traditional Chinese residences. The most representative types are *taimen* and water-side residences. *Taimen* is a kind of multi-courtyard residence of wealthy families in the past, usually consisting of two-storied buildings around small courtyards. The halls and parlors have low windows in the front and rear, and conventional wooden structures. High quality building materials are used, with luxurious decoration such as the distinctive woodcarvings in Dongyang residences in Zhejiang Province. The waterside residence is a representative residence of common people. As the Jiangsu and Zhejiang areas abound with rivers and streams, boats used to be an indispensable means of transport, and residences were built next to the water. A common residence is flanked by a stream and a street, with a private dock by the water for mooring boats and washing vegetables and rice.

The Water Compound in Pengxi Village dates from the Ming Dynasty. It was built around a pool.

Residences in Nanxijiang stress a harmonious combination of architecture and water. The picture shows the Water and Moon Building, which stands in the center of a pool in Cangpo Village.

Dongyang in Zhejiang Province is famous for the carvings on the wooden frames of its buildings.

A latticed wall in the Yunshan Building near Pengxi Village, decorated with exquisite brick carvings. It is a masterpiece of its kind.

Residences by the water in Zhouzhuang, Suzhou, Jiangsu Province.

Red-brick Dwellings in Quanzhou

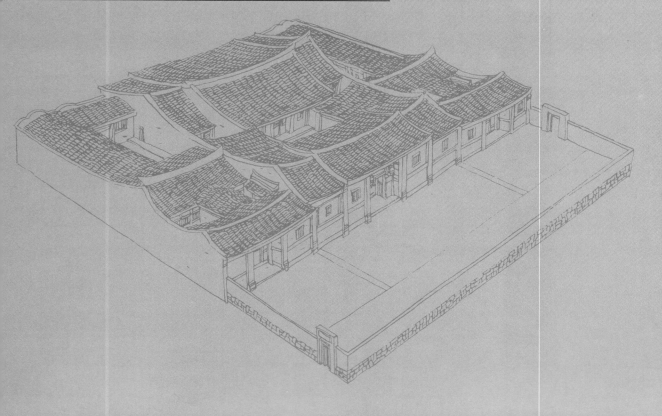

Unlike most solemn, elegant Chinese houses built with gray bricks and tiles, the houses near Quanzhou in Fujian Province are built with red bricks and tiles. The Zhangli Village of Guanqiao Township in Nan'an County, Fujian Province is a well-preserved traditional village with red brick residences. A bird's view of the village will show red roofs properly spaced.

The stone carvings in Quanzhou residences are intricate and striking.

The quadrangle is the main form of residence in Quanzhou, which retains many characteristics of the residences in the Central Plain before the Song Dynasty (960-1279), such as spacious rooms, symmetrical layout and comparatively low ceilings.

Brick and stone carvings are widely used in Quanzhou residences. In addition to the large brick and stone carvings at the entrance, the inside is decorated with pierced stone carvings as windows. The patterns are mostly realistic, detailed images of plants and human beings, displaying a strong worldly flavor.

A bird's-eye view of a courtyard dwelling in Quanzhou.

Earthen Buildings in Fujian Province

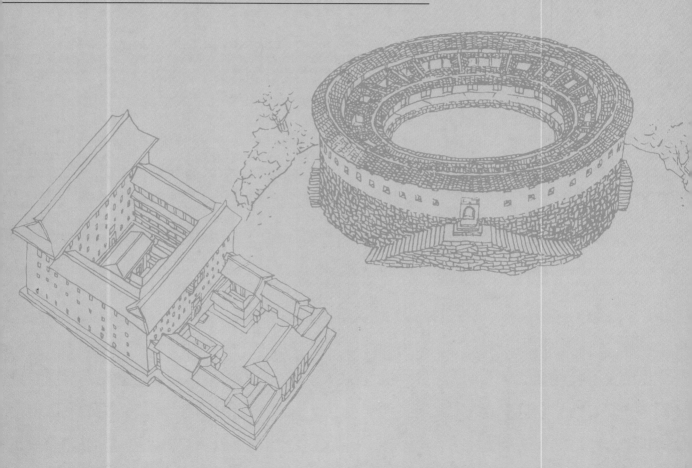

Round earthen buildings can be divided into two types: the compound consisting of separate residences and the compound consisting of connected residences. Most compounds are of the latter type, like those in Yongding and Nanjing counties. The picture shows an earthen compound in Xiaxi Village, Chuyang Township, Yongding County.

The most famous residence in Fujian is the earthen building, especially the round type. Foreign experts, deeply impressed, call it "a unique form of abode in mountainous areas." The earthen building is mainly distributed in remote mountainous areas where the Hakkas inhabit, including Yongding County, the west part of Nanjing County and the south part of Longyan County. Yongding County has the largest number of earthen buildings. There are 7,000 square earthen buildings and 300 round ones in the county, all three-storied and higher, and over 50 years old.

A group of earthen buildings in Yongding, Fujian Province.

Fujian earthen buildings vary in shapes. There are single earthen buildings, and square, round, swastika-shaped and half-moon-shaped earthen buildings. Single earthen buildings, mostly found in Yongding County, feature large, hip-and-gable roofs, large eaves, and trapezoidal walls. Single earthen buildings can be combined into complexes in various shapes. The "Minister's Residence" Wenyi Hall in the Fuling Village in Gaobei Township in Yongding County, locally known as "Building of Five Phoenixes," is an example of the combination. It consists of five buildings, three of which form three rows, the front lower than the rear, extending from east to west, flanked by the other two buildings extending from north to south, thus forming a layout in the shape of the Chinese character "sun." The Wenji Hall is a perfect building, displaying an antique, solemn, magnificent style. The layout is orderly and neat, with the main and subsidiary buildings clearly distinguished and harmoniously combined.

View of the inside of the Zhencheng Compound in Hongkeng Township, Yongding County.

A lane between a square compound and a round compound.

The Umbrella Compound in Gaoche
Township, Hua'an County.

The earthen buildings in Fushi Township, Yongding County, are large and magnificent. The picture shows the Yonglongchang Compound at Xinzhaiba, Fushi, a large earthen compound with separate buildings and divided into the new and old parts. There are 92 halls, 624 rooms, 144 staircases and seven wells. The main building has six stories.

The Yongqing Compound in Zhangpu County looks like a windmill.

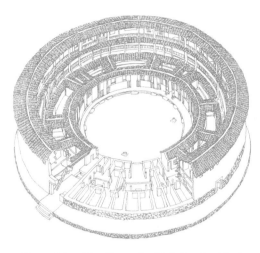

The round-shaped Eryi Compound in Dadi Township, Hua'an County, Fujian Province is a large compound consisting of separate residences. It is ingeniously designed and very practical.

A bird's-eye view of an earthen compound.

Fortified Compound in Southern Jiangxi Province

Fortified compounds in southern Jiangxi vary in shape, form and building material. The setting of the watchtowers is also flexible. The picture shows a fortified compound in Longnan County, with watchtowers built at the four corners.

and imposing. One has to pass three gates to enter the compound: the iron outer gate, the middle lock gate and the wooden inner gate. Each gate has openings for pouring water, so as to defend the village from fire attacks. Originally the compound had a large courtyard in the center, with wells and cellars for storing grains. Later some one-storied houses were built in it. In addition to the corner towers, the compound has loopholes on each floor, so that the enemies are unable to get near the village from any direction. The top floor contains a corridor, which facilitates movements of military men during a battle.

The fortified compound in southern Jiangxi Province are similar to the Fujian square earth buildings in shape, and usually have corner towers like the fortified buildings in Kaiping, Guangdong Province. In the Yangcun Township, Longnan County, there are three famous fortified compounds: Yanyi, Yongzhuang and Guangyi.

The Yanyi Fortified Compound, well preserved today, is the largest and of the best quality in the three. The gray brick exterior walls look solid

The picture shows a well designed watchtower at one corner of a building in Longnan County, with loopholes opening to various directions.

A well outside the Dongsheng Fortified Compound in Anyuan County.

A fortified compound usually contains scores of households, or several hundred people. All major matters are handled by the head of the village in accordance with tradition. The picture shows the new Fortified Compound in Xintian Village, Egong Township, Dingnan County.

The inside of the Yanyi Fortified Compound.

The U-shaped Compounds of the Hakka

A U-shaped compound of the Hakka People in Nankou Township, Meixian County, Guangdong Province.

In the innumerable verdant hills in Meixian County, Guangdong Province lie patches of rice fields and residences. Most residences are in a U-shaped compound, facing a half-moon-shaped pond and the fields, and usually with a woods or slope in the rear. Containing scores to over a hundred rooms, the compounds are not uniform in shape.

The U-shaped compounds are rammed earth buildings. The 30 cm thick walls were built with the mixture of lime, mud, sand and a proper quantity of sticky rice and brown sugar. Such walls are solid and more enduring than cement walls. It takes several years to build a multi-storied compound. In Meixian, there are some U-shaped compounds built several hundred years ago, of which the walls are so solid that it is hard to hammer a nail into them. The high-quality, two-storied Nanhuayou Villa in Meixian, built in 1904, consists of 10 halls, nine wells and 108 rooms. The magnificent building contains many Western architectural and decorative methods. The U-shaped compounds of the Hakkas in Meixian are a product of the history and social conditions, which met the needs of living, defense and production during that time.

This is the two-storied Yu'an Villa built by Hakka people in Nankou Township, Meixian County.

The partitions, doors and windows in the U-shaped compounds in Meixian bear exquisite woodcarvings with local flavors and in a style far different from those in the other parts of the county.

The semicircular courtyard in a typical U-shaped compound looks like the back of a turtle, with its center gently bulging upward.

A bird's-eye view of the Nanhuayou Villa in Nankou Township, Meixian County.

Fortified Buildings in Kaiping

In China, residential buildings in different areas have different characteristics, and it is hard to say which is orthodox. In Kaiping, Guangdong Province, one can see conventional Chinese residences with courtyards and fortified buildings with Western characteristics. The latter bear more local colors. In history, Kaiping suffered from social turmoil and floods. Starting from the early years of the Qing Dynasty (1644-1911), people built fortified buildings to protect themselves from flooding and theft.

A fortified building in Changsha Township, Kaiping County, Guangdong Province. The architect stressed the decoration on the upper part of the building.

A fortified building in Kaiping with a peculiar top.

A fortified building in Kaiping

The fortified buildings in Kaiping show combinations of Chinese and Western architectural styles.

Flagstone Buildings in Guizhou Province

The Buyei people in the Anshun area generally live in flagstone houses.

Located in the east part of the Yunnan-Guizhou Plateau, Guizhou is well known for its hilly terrain. In Anyang and Guiyang, where there are rocky mountains, flagstone buildings are the representative residences. In fact, a flagstone building is not entirely built with stones, but a wooden structure wrapped in stone walls and a stone roof. The roofing is unique, with 2 cm thick stone plates serving as tiles.

Ingenious arrangement of stone plates.

The exterior of a residence built entirely with flagstones.

Typical residences in Shibanshao Township, Huaxi District, Guiyang.

Residential Buildings of the Koreans

Most Korean residences are detached, with a courtyard enclosed by a low fence. Most houses have a hipped roof.

    The residences of the Koreans in northeast China are very characteristic. Most residences have a hipped thatch roof. The hip-and-gable roof is only found on tile-roofed houses. Large hip tiles are used, so the Korean residences have obviously wide ridges. The Korean residences have a fixed layout, generally consisting of six or eight rooms.

The interior of a Korean house is low, and the family sleeps on the heated floor. The picture shows a central room, with the kitchen in the forefront. Rooms are separated by sliding doors.

Mongolian Yurts

Mongolian yurts are grouped according to family ties. The nomadic Mongolian herdsmen still live in yurts.

Mongolian yurts, a peculiar form of residence in China, have developed into perfectness in its history of over two millennia. A Mongolian yurt covers a circular area, and fronts the east where the sun rises, thus preventing the west wind from blowing into the yurt, especially in the cold winter. The longitudinal section of the yurt is a vault, which enables a light latticework frame to support several layers of felts. The streamline shape of the yurt reduces the force of the wind from any direction.

It takes less than half an hour to set up a yurt.

The interior of a yurt is closely arranged. A stove stands in the center, surrounded by furniture. The other parts of the floor are covered with carpets, and this is where people sit and sleep.

Residential Buildings of the Uygurs

A residence with adobe walls in Turpan.

Residences of the Uygurs are spacious and flexible, partitioned with earth lattice walls and arch doors. As the temperature varies much between day and night, reaching as high as 47°C during the day and 20°C during the night in summer, the residences have extra thick walls and generally no side windows, but front windows or skylights. Because of the windiness in the area, the houses are built close to one another, with small courtyards.

In the Turpan Depression where rain is rare throughout the year, people generally live in houses with a wooden frame and adobe walls. Only rich families live in brick houses.

In Kashi, where the land for construction is limited, people generally live in multi-storied buildings. The Uygurs build their toilets on the roofs, so that the feces dry up quickly in the dry weather and can be disposed of with a spade. Houses in Kashi and Hotan may face any direction. The interior has many niches, and is splendidly decorated with plaster or plywood relief works.

A decorated porch in a courtyard in Yining City.

Decorated niches in a residence in Kashi.

The Kawakqa House in Hotan, Xinjiang.

A village of the Aini people, a branch of the Hani.

Yunnan and Guizhou in southwest China attract tourists with their beautiful scenery. Various styles of houses are as interesting as the scenery. The national minorities inhabiting these areas include the Dongs, Miaos, Dais, Jingpos, Vas, Hanis and Shuis. Some of the people live in houses on stilts, which have a long history.

Houses on stilts are built with bamboo or wood, the space under the house serves as a livestock pen or storeroom. There are houses on high stilts and on low stilts. The interior of such a house does not have good lighting, but well ventilated. The large eaves block solar radiation. The stilts lift the house from the damp ground. In sparsely populated areas, such a house protects the residents against beasts.

The drum tower and typical residences of the Dong people of Ma'an Village, Sanjiang County, in the Guangxi Zhuang Autonomous Region. The drum tower, village gate, stage for performances and bridge are common public installations in a Dong village.

A stilted residence of the Jino people in the Youle Mountains, Jinghong County, Yunnan Province.

Qianjia Village in Leishan County, Guizhou Province, is a large Dong village. In its center stands a tall drum tower.

Dai bamboo houses in Xishuangbanna, Yunnan Province

Residential Buildings in Lijiang

A traditional lane in Lijiang, with three shallow wells arranged on three levels: The higher one is for drinking, the middle one for washing vegetables, and the lower one for washing clothes.

The beautiful ancient city of Lijiang in Yunnan Province, located near the bordering areas of Yunnan, Sichuan and Tibet, is the home place of the Naxis. Streams run across the city. The houses, built by the streams or over the streams, combine Han, Bai and Tibetan architectural styles.

A street in Lijiang.

A gate in the shape of a memorial arch in Lijiang.

Exquisite patterns on the paved courtyard of a residence in Lijiang.

A bird's-eye view of the ancient city of Lijiang.

The Houses of the Bai

A corner structure in the shape of a revolving lantern over the lower eaves.

Residences of the Bais are famous for their colorful, exquisite decoration and graceful shapes. With characteristics peculiar to the Bais, they suit the windy climate and frequent earthquakes. Typical forms of the Bais' residences are a courtyard with two-storied buildings on three sides and a screen wall on the other and rectangular five-courtyard houses. The Bais believe that a house should have a hill in the rear, instead of a gully or a clearing, which is inauspicious.

The gates of Bai residences vary in shape. A gate like this, without eaves, is rare.

A triple-part screen wall.

A bird's-eye view of Bai residences. The lane leads to a courtyard house with buildings on three sides of the courtyard and a screen wall on the other. A part of the screen wall can be seen.

Tibetan Fortified Manor Houses

An aerial view shows that the Tibetan residences are arranged in neat square shapes, surrounded by stone walls. Large windows usually open onto a courtyard.

Fortified manor houses are a common form of residence in agricultural areas, cities and towns on the Qinghai-Tibet Plateau and in some parts of Inner Mongolia. The three- or four-story-high houses are built with irregular stones or earth, and look like blockhouses.

In the past, the common Tibetan people lived in crude, flat-roofed one-story houses built with stones and earth, while aristocrats, lords and rich merchants lived in fortified manor houses of three to five stories. The fortified manor houses have a courtyard and enclosing walls of about 66 cm thick that serves as a defense in battles. Most windows open toward the courtyard, and the windows and doors opening to the outside are small and narrow, so as to keep out the wind and cold. The second and third floors are the living parts, while the ground floor serves as a storage. The pillars and beams are decorated with beautiful paintings. The best room in the center is the hall for worshipping Buddha.

In many agricultural areas in Tibet, common farmers live in similar houses, which are of two or three stories, covering a rectangular area. One enters through the door into the ground floor, which serves as a livestock pen, and climbs up a wooden ladder to the second floor,where people live. The third floor contains a hall for worshipping Buddha and a grain storage.

Residences in Sa'gya are typical of those of the Tibetans.

The home of Nyima, a Tibetan doctor, in Jiesha Village, Zethang Township in Tibet, is elegantly furnished. This is the gate of her house.

The interior of a Tibetan residence in Deqin, Yunnan Province.

A traditional window.

Residences near the Samya Monastery in Zethang, Tibet. Multistoried buildings form courtyard residences.

Appendix

Locations of Major Types of Chinese Residences

1. The Courtyard Houses of Beijing   2. Residences in Qixian County, Shanxi Province   3. Cave Dwellings
4. Residential Buildings in Southern Anhui Province   5. Residential Buildings in the Southern Region of Rivers and Lakes
6. Red-brick Dwellings in Quanzhou   7. Earthen Buildings in Fujian Province   8. Fortified Compound in Southern Jiangxi Province
9. The U-shaped Compounds of the Hakka   10. Fortified Buildings in Kaiping   11. Flagstone Buildings in Guizhou Province
12. Residential Buildings of the Koreans   13. Mongolian Yurts   14. Residential Buildings of the Uygurs
15. Houses on Stilts   16. Residential Buildings in Lijiang   17. The Houses of the Bai   18. Tibetan Fortified Manor Houses

图书在版编目（CIP）数据

中国传统民居／王其钧编著．－北京：外文出版社，2002.5
（中华风物）
ISBN 7-119-03041-8

Ⅰ．中…Ⅱ．王…Ⅲ．民居－中国－图集　Ⅳ.TU241.5-64
中国版本图书馆 CIP 数据核字(2002)第 022507 号

"中华风物"编辑委员会

顾　　问：蔡名照　赵常谦　黄友义　刘质彬
主　　编：肖晓明
编　　委：肖晓明　李振国　田　辉　呼宝珉
　　　　　房永明　胡开敏　崔黎丽　兰佩瑾

责任编辑：贾先锋
撰　　文：王其钧　贾先锋
英文翻译：张韶宁
英文审定：王增芬
摄　　影：王其钧　兰佩瑾　孙树明　成卫东
　　　　　李植森　余志勇　孙建平
内文设计：唐少文
封面设计：蔡　荣

中国传统民居

王其钧　著

© 外文出版社
外文出版社出版
（中国北京百万庄大街 24 号）
邮政编码：100037
外文出版社网页：http://www.flp.com.cn
外文出版社电子邮件地址：info@flp.com.cn
sales@flp.com.cn
北京大容彩色印刷有限公司印刷
中国国际图书贸易总公司发行
（中国北京车公庄西路 35 号）
北京邮政信箱第 399 号　邮政编码　100044
2002 年(24 开)第 1 版
2004 年第 1 版第 2 次印刷
（英）
ISBN 7-119-03041-8/J.1595（外）
05800（平）
85-E-530P